THE POCKET FIBRE COUNTER

FREDERICK MULLER LTD
LONDON SW19 7JZ

Published in 1982 by
Frederick Muller Ltd
Dataday House
Wimbledon, London SW19 7JZ

ISBN 0 584 40001 2

Printed by Devon Print Group, Exeter

Acknowledgements

The publishers gratefully acknowledge the use of
information from McCance and Widdowson's
Composition of Foods by A.A. Paul and
D.A.T. Southgate, published by H.M.S.O., and
from the manufacturers who have supplied data for
this book.

Although every effort has been made to ensure the
accuracy of the tables in this book it cannot be
guaranteed.

INTRODUCTION

Recent investigations have provided evidence that most of us in the developed countries of the world should considerably increase the amount of high-fibre food in our diet.

In the past, when meat, refined grains and sugar were regarded as a special treat, we consumed a great deal of fibre in a high carbohydrate diet. As we have become more affluent, and as technology has improved food production techniques in the Western world, our consumption of meat and dairy proteins, refined grains, sugar and easily digested convenience foods has increased enormously.

We have consequently neglected "whole foods", which have been relegated to health food shops, to be purchased only by "cranks". We believed that it was the protein, vitamins and minerals that mattered, and, because fibre wasn't absorbed into the body, it had no food value.

These ideas began to change when doctors working in third world countries noticed that much of the population existed quite happily on what we would consider a very poor diet, based on carbohydrates obtained from whole grains, root vegetables, beans and fruit.

Even more amazing was the fact not only that these people appeared to be quite adequately nourished, but also that many of the medical conditions increasing at an alarming rate in the West were unknown in these countries.

Further studies convinced some scientists that if we increased our fibre intake considerably it could help us to avoid many typically western illnesses such as constipation, obesity, diverticular disease, some forms of diabetes, hiatus hernia, haemorrhoids, varicose veins, gallstones and possibly even appendicitis.

WHAT IS DIETARY FIBRE?

Dietary fibre has proved to be a much more complex ingredient of our diet than previously recognised. It is not "roughage", whatever that was, and it is not "crude fibre", a term used to describe that part of food which remains undigested when treated with dilute acid and alkali. Figures given for crude fibre underestimate the total dietary fibre in a food.

Dietary fibre consists of different components—cellulose, non-cellulosic polysaccharides and lignin—which occur in foods of vegetable origin. The proportions of the different constituents vary from one plant to another, and as the different constituents probably have different functions, various sources of fibre should be included in the diet.

Dietary fibre increases stool weight because it absorbs water and encourages the growth of bacteria. Fibre-bound water may also dilute toxins in the body. The various functions of fibre in the body are still being investigated but there is strong evidence that it can relieve and prevent a number of disorders.

RELIEF OF CONSTIPATION

Constipation is an extremely common complaint in Western societies and virtually unknown in underdeveloped countries. In Britain alone we consume 40,000 gallons of liquid paraffin a year and issue five million prescriptions for laxatives, besides all the over-the-counter purchases of purgatives of various kinds.

Doctors quite rightly discourage the use of laxatives, which provide only short term relief and can cause long-term medical problems. Until recently the medical profession advised that a daily bowel movement was unnecessary and that we should let nature take its course. Nature, however, cannot take its course on the type of diet we have become used to in the West.

Because fibre increases stool weight, it prevents and relieves constipation. In Britain it is estimated that we eat between 10 and 15 grammes of fibre a day, and this needs to be at least doubled in order to prevent constipation, which is the basis of many other medical problems.

PREVENTION OF OBESITY

One of the most exciting recent findings is that a high-fibre diet can help to prevent obesity and is of great benefit in any slimming regime. In any attempt to lose weight it is, of course, essential to limit one's calorie intake, but it has been found that the inclusion of many high-fibre foods in the diet can help the slimmer in various ways.

Foods rich in dietary fibre take longer to chew and to swallow than less fibrous foods, and it is known that the slower one eats the less food one is likely to eat before one is full.

Because fibre-rich foods are comparatively bulky for the amount of energy-producing calories they contain, they provide more bulk in the stomach, giving a feeling of fullness. They also stay in the stomach longer because high-fibre foods are more difficult to digest than refined foods.

On the other hand, once the food leaves the stomach it travels on quickly and easily, so avoiding constipation and its other associated medical problems.

Perhaps the most encouraging new finding for slimmers is that it appears that those on high-fibre diets excrete measureably more calories than those on a typical Western diet. This means that weight is lost not only by eating less calories but also by excreting them. The fibre part of a food is not digested at all and therefore provides no calories, but it is believed that some of the nutritious elements of fibrous food are excreted along with the indigestible cell walls.

DIVERTICULAR DISEASE

Diverticula are small protrusions of mucous membrane which bulge out through a weak part of the bowel wall. It is estimated that these are present in about one third of people aged 60 and over in Great Britain. In about 10% of these cases the surrounding tissue becomes infected and inflamed causing acute pain. Abscesses and peritonitis can follow.

Diverticulosis (the condition where diverticula are present) is practically unknown in Africa and Asia and was extremely rare in the West until early in the twentieth century. The disease is believed to be caused by intra-abdominal pressure caused by chronic constipation over a long period, and can be prevented by a high-fibre diet. It has also been shown that almost all cases can be relieved by such a diet and that, if followed, complications requiring surgery should no longer occur.

COLON CANCER

Cancer of the colon is the second most lethal cancer in Britain today and there is strong evidence that it is associated with a low-fibre diet. It may be that fibre has a protective action against carcinogens in the colon, or that the fibre-bound water dilutes the toxins. A high-fibre diet also removes these potentially dangerous toxins from the body more quickly.

HEART DISEASE

It is known that citrus pectin, which is part of the fibre contained in fruit, lowers blood cholesterol, and studies have also shown that those who eat a great deal of cereal fibre are less likely to have coronary heart attacks than those on a low-fibre diet. There is as yet no conclusive evidence, but there are strong indications that our present low-fibre diet may be linked with the high incidence of coronary heart disease in the West.

A high-fibre diet is also bound to contain less animal fat which has been linked with heart disease.

DIABETES

The form of diabetes that starts in later life is very rare among peoples with a high-fibre intake, and it is believed to be caused by a diet that is low in dietary fibre. Because high-fibre carbohydrates are absorbed by the body more slowly than refined carbohydrates, a high-fibre diet is now recommended in the treatment of this sort of diabetes.

PRESSURE PHENOMENA

Fibre-deficient diets have also been implicated in haemorrhoids, varicose vains and hiatus hernia. Abdominal pressur caused by constipation may be the cause.

HOW MUCH FIBRE

It is estimated that the average Briton consumes about 1 grammes of fibre a day—which is one of the lowest figure for fibre consumption in the world. This is an average figur and many people, especially those on low-carbohydrate slim ming diets, consume less than this.

A typical low-carbohydrate slimming menu might consist c the following.

Breakfast:	Orange Juice	0 fibre
	Boiled Egg	0 fibre
	1 slice Slimmers Bread	1.4g fibre
Lunch:	Ham	0 fibre
	Salad—lettuce	
	Tomato, Cucumber	1.4g fibre
	2 Starch-Reduced	
	Crispbreads	1.8g fibre
	Yogurt	0 fibre
Dinner:	Roast Chicken	0 fibre
	3 oz Cauliflower	1.5g fibre
	3 oz Carrots	2.7g fibre
	4 oz Grapes	0.9g fibre
		7.7g fibre

This menu may appear to be very healthy but it contains half the amount of fibre consumed by the average person in Great Britain, and the average amount is less than half that recommended for good health.

In Africa and Asia the average figure is more like 50 grammes a day and more than 100 grammes are consumed by some groups. This very high intake of over 100 grammes is probably excessive and may prevent adequate nutrients and energy being obtained from the diet.

If we in the West aimed at consuming between 35 and 50 grammes of fibre a day, it is likely that we could avoid many of the illnesses mentioned earlier, and in addition stay slim, or lose weight if calories are also controlled.

HOW TO EAT MORE FIBRE

Dietary fibre is found in varying amounts in foods of vegetable origin. Meat, fish, eggs and dairy products contain no fibre—they are an important source of protein but we tend to eat too much of them, neglecting vegetable products, many of which also contain protein.

The tables in this book will provide surprises. The texture of a food is no guide to the amount of fibre it contains. A salad of lettuce, tomato, celery and cucumber appears to be fibrous, but those vegetables usually considered as salad ingredients are, in fact, mostly water. It would be necessary to eat more than 20 oz of cucumber to obtain the amount of fibre found in 1 oz of baked beans.

It is not difficult to consume 50 grammes of dietary fibre a day if we use the following tables carefully and are prepared to change our eating habits a little. Consider the menu below.

Breakfast:	1 oz Bran Buds	8g fibre
	1 Banana	3.4g fibre
Lunch:	8 oz Baked Beans	16.8g fibre
	1 Slice Wholemeal Toast	2.8g fibre
	1 Orange	2.1g fibre
Dinner:	Slice of Melon	1.6g fibre
	Grilled Chicken Piece	0 fibre
	Baked Potato (6 oz)	4.2g fibre
	4 oz Peas	6g fibre
	4 oz Carrots	3.6g fibre
	Baked Apple	3.4g fibre
	½ oz Sultanas	1 fibre
		52.9g fibre

This very satisfying menu contains over 50 grammes of fibre and approximately 1000 calories, not including any extras such as milk in drinks etc. As most people need to consume more than 1000 calories a day, the planning of a high-fibre diet, using the information in this book, should not be a problem.

Note
Values are given for raw and cooked weights where these are available. The fibre content of a food is not changed by cooking but the weight is altered and therefore the amount of fibre per 100 grammes.

Values for stewed fruits are without added sugar.

Food	Measure	Fibre (g)	Calories
ALL-BRAN	100g	27.9	248
	1oz	7.9	70
ALMONDS			
Kernels only	100g	14.3	565
	1oz	4.1	160
Weighed with shells	100g	5.3	210
	1oz	1.5	59
ALMOND PASTE	100g	6.4	443
	1oz	1.8	126
ALPEN	100g	6.8	424
	1oz	1.9	120
APPLES			
Eating, with skin	100g	2.0	35
	Av. fruit (4oz)	2.3	40
Cooking, *baked*	100g	2.0	31
	Av. fruit (6oz)	3.4	53
stewed	100g	2.1	32
	1oz	0.6	9

Food	Measure	Fibre (g)	Calories
APRICOTS			
Fresh	100g	1.9	25
	1oz	0.5	7
Dried, *raw*	100g	24.0	182
	1oz	6.8	52
stewed	100g	8.9	66
	1oz	2.5	19
Canned, *with syrup*	100g	1.3	223
	1oz	0.4	63
ASPARAGUS TIPS			
boiled	100g	1.5	18
	1oz	0.4	5
boiled, weighed as served	100g	0.8	9
	1oz	0.2	3
AUBERGINE			
raw	100g	2.5	14
	1oz	0.7	4
AVOCADO PEARS			
flesh only	100g	2.0	223
	1oz	0.6	63

Food	Measure	Fibre (g)	Calories
BAKED BEANS			
Canned in tomato sauce	100g	7.3	64
	1oz	2.1	18
	8oz can	16.8	145
BANANAS			
raw	100g	3.4	79
	1oz	1.0	22
raw, weighed with skin	100g	2.0	47
	Av. fruit	3.4	80
BARCELONA NUTS			
Kernels only	100g	10.3	639
	1oz	2.9	181
Weighed with shells	100g	6.4	396
	1oz	1.8	112
BARLEY			
raw	100g	6.5	360
	1oz	1.8	102
boiled	100g	2.2	120
	1oz	0.6	34
BEANS			
BAKED			
Canned in tomato sauce	100g	7.3	64
	1oz	2.1	18
BROAD			
boiled	100g	4.2	48
	1oz	1.2	14

Food	Measure	Fibre (g)	Calories
BUTTER			
raw	100g	21.6	273
	1oz	6.1	77
boiled	100g	5.1	95
	1oz	1.4	27
FRENCH			
boiled	100g	3.2	7
	1oz	0.9	2
HARICOT			
raw	100g	25.4	271
	1oz	7.2	77
boiled	100g	7.5	93
	1oz	2.1	26
MUNG			
raw	100g	22.0	231
	1oz	6.2	65
cooked, dahl	100g	6.4	106
	1oz	1.8	30
RED KIDNEY			
raw	100g	25.0	272
	1oz	7.1	77

Food	Measure	Fibre (g)	Calories
RUNNER			
raw	100g	2.9	26
	1oz	0.8	7
boiled	100g	3.4	19
	1oz	1.0	5
BEANSPROUTS			
Canned	100g	3.0	9
	1oz	0.9	3
BEETROOT			
raw	100g	3.1	28
	1oz	0.9	8
boiled	100g	2.5	44
	1oz	0.7	12
BEMAX			
Crunchy	100g	14.5	321
	1oz	4.1	91
BISCUITS			
Sweet			
CHOCOLATE, full–coated	100g	3.1	524
	1oz	0.9	149
CUSTARD CREAMS	100g	1.2	513
	1oz	0.3	145
DIGESTIVE, plain	100g	5.5	471
	1oz	1.6	135
chocolate	100g	3.5	493
	1oz	1.0	140

Food	Measure	Fibre (g)	Calories
GINGERNUTS	100g	2.0	456
	1oz	0.6	129
LINCOLN	100g	1.7	469
	1oz	0.5	133
MARIE	100g	2.3	457
	1oz	0.7	130
OATCAKES	100g	4.0	441
	1oz	1.1	125
OSBORNE	100g	2.3	457
	1oz	0.7	130
RICH TEA	100g	2.3	457
	1oz	0.7	130
SHORTCAKE	100g	1.7	469
	1oz	0.5	133
SHORTBREAD	100g	2.1	504
	1oz	0.6	143
WAFERS	100g	1.6	535
	1oz	0.5	152
Plain			
CREAM CRACKERS	100g	3.0	440
	1oz	0.9	125
MATZOS	100g	3.9	384
	1oz	1.1	109

Food	Measure	Fibre (g)	Calories
WATER BISCUITS	100g	3.2	440
	1oz	0.9	125
SPECIALIST BRANDS			
Allinson			
BRAN BISCUITS	100g	7.4	496
	1oz	2.1	141
BRAN OATCAKES	100g	11.0	419
	1oz	3.1	119
COCONUT BISCUITS	100g	7.7	524
	1oz	2.2	149
FRUIT AND NUT BISCUITS	100g	4.7	524
	1oz	1.3	149
GINGER BISCUITS	100g	4.4	398
	1oz	1.2	113
HONEY BISCUITS	100g	5.8	436
	1oz	1.6	124
MUESLI BISCUITS	100g	4.6	409
	1oz	1.3	116

Food	Measure	Fibre (g)	Calories
OATMEAL BISCUITS	100g	4.5	507
	1oz	1.3	144
SPICE BISCUITS	100g	4.7	534
	1oz	1.3	151
WALNUT BISCUITS	100g	3.7	442
	1oz	1.0	125
WHOLEMEAL SHORTBREAD	100g	7.0	494
	1oz	2.0	140
Energen STARCH REDUCED SWEETMEAL DIGESTIVE	100g	4.0	475
	1oz	1.1	135
Itona GRANNY ANN HI-FI BISCUITS	100g	5.7	350
	1oz	1.6	99
BLACKBERRIES			
raw	100g	7.3	29
	1oz	2.1	8
stewed	100g	6.3	25
	1oz	1.8	8
canned	100g	4.2	83
	1oz	1.2	23
BLACKCURRANTS			
raw	100g	8.7	28
	1oz	2.5	8

Food	Measure	Fibre (g)	Calories
stewed	100g	7.4	24
	1oz	2.1	7
canned	100g	5.0	81
	1oz	1.4	23
BRAN	100g	44.0	206
	1oz	12.5	58
BRAN PLUS *(Allinson)*	100g	25.0	222
	1oz	7.1	63
BRAN, BROAD *(Allinson)*	100g	44.0	152
	1oz	12.5	43
BRAN BUDS *(Kelloggs)*	100g	28.2	245
	1oz	8.0	72
BRANCRISP *(Energen)*	100g	20.0	350
	each	1.3	23
BRAN CRUNCH *(Energen)*	100g	15.0	412
	1oz	4.3	110
BRAN FLAKES *(Kelloggs)*	100g	11.8	315
	1oz	3.3	89

Food	Measure	Fibre (g)	Calories
BRAN MUESLI *(Prewetts)*	100g	22.0	308
	1oz	6.2	87
BRAZIL NUTS			
Kernels only	100g	9.0	619
	1oz	2.6	175
Weighed with shells	100g	4.1	277
	1oz	1.2	78
BREAD			
WHOLEMEAL	100g	8.5	216
	1oz	2.4	61
BROWN	100g	5.1	223
	1oz	1.4	63
WHITE	100g	2.7	233
	1oz	0.8	66
Nimble			
FAMILY WHITE	100g	2.8	278
	1 slice	0.5	50
FARMSTEAD	100g	8.5	252
	1 slice	1.2	40
GRANARY	100g	6.1	277
	1 slice	0.9	41
STANDARD BROWN	100g	4.4	272
	1 slice	0.5	35

Food	Measure	Fibre (g)	Calories
STANDARD WHITE	100g	2.8	278
	1 slice	0.4	35
Procea WHITE AND BROWN	100g	2.6	231
	1 slice	0.4	36
Slimcea WHITE AND BROWN	100g	2.5	244
	1 slice	0.3	32
Sunblest HIBRAN	100g	11.1	202
	1 slice	2.0	38
Vitbe WHEATGERM	100g	4.8	231
	1 slice	1.7	81

Windmill BRAN LOAF	100g	6.3	204
	1 lge slice	2.0	66
COUNTRY BROWN	100g	5.7	215
	1 lge slice	1.8	70

Food	Measure	Fibre (g)	Calories
GRANARY	100g	6.8	218
	1 small slice	1.7	55
HIGH FIBRE WHITE	100g	5.7	222
	1 lge slice	1.8	72
WHOLEMEAL	100g	8.6	202
	1 lge slice	2.8	66
BREAD MIXES **Allinson**			
BRAN BREAD MIX	100g	13.2	361
	1 pack	74.8	2046
MALT BREAD MIX	100g	2.5	328
	1 pack	14.2	1859
WHITE BREAD MIX	100g	3.2	351
	1 pack	18.1	1990
WHOLEWHEAT BREAD MIX	100g	10.0	329
	1 pack	56.7	1865

Food	Measure	Fibre (g)	Calories
Prewetts			
BRAN BREAD MIX	100g	13.2	311
	1 pack	74.8	1763
BROWN BREAD MIX	100g	9.4	336
	1 pack	53.2	1905
EVERREADY BREAD MIX	100g	8.5	334
	1 pack	48.2	1894
WHITE BREAD MIX	100g	3.2	346
	1 pack	18.1	1962
BREAD ROLLS			
BROWN, *crusty*	100g	5.9	289
	1oz	1.7	82
soft	100g	5.4	282
	1oz	1.5	80
WHITE, *crusty*	100g	3.1	290
	1oz	0.9	82
soft	100g	2.9	305
	1oz	0.8	86
Energen STARCH REDUCED ROLLS	100g	2.0	384
	each	0.1	24
BREAKFAST CEREALS			
ALL-BRAN *(Kelloggs)*	100g	27.9	248
	1oz	7.9	70

Food	Measure	Fibre (g)	Calories
ALPEN *(Weetabix)*	100g	6.8	424
	1oz	1.9	120
BRAN BUDS *(Kelloggs)*	100g	28.2	254
	1oz	8.0	72
BRAN CRUNCH *(Energen)*	100g	15.0	412
	1oz	4.3	110
BRAN FLAKES *(Kelloggs)*	100g	11.8	315
	1oz	3.3	89
BRAN MUESLI *(Prewetts)*	100g	22.0	308
	1oz	6.2	87
CORN FLAKES *(Kelloggs)*	100g	8.9	344
	1oz	2.5	97
COUNTRY STORE *(Kelloggs)*	100g	5.1	352
	1oz	1.4	100
CRACKLIN' BRAN *(Kelloggs)*	100g	10.5	387
	1oz	3.0	110

Food	Measure	Fibre (g)	Calories
GOLDEN GRAINS *(Prewetts)*	100g	5.5	376
	1oz	1.6	107
GRAPENUTS *(General Foods)*	100g	7.0	355
	1oz	2.0	101
HONEY BRAN *(Allinson)*	100g	27.0	248
	1oz	7.6	70
HONEY MUESLI *(Prewetts)*	100g	6.4	366
	1oz	1.8	104
MUESLI *(Prewetts)*	100g	6.8	359
	1oz	1.9	102
MUESLI DELUXE *(Prewetts)*	100g	7.4	390
	1oz	2.1	111
ORIGINAL CRUNCHY *with Honey, Almonds and Raisins (Jordans)*	100g	4.7	426
	1oz	1.3	121
ORIGINAL CRUNCHY *with Bran and Apple (Jordans)*	100g	10.2	410
	1oz	2.9	116
PUFFED WHEAT *(Quaker)*	100g	15.4	3?5
	1oz	4.4	

Food	Measure	Fibre (g)	Calories
QUICK QUAKER OATS	100g	6.0	359
With Bran	1oz	1.7	102
READY BREK *(Lyons)*	100g	7.6	390
	1oz	2.2	111
RICE KRISPIES *(Kelloggs)*	100g	4.0	352
	1oz	1.1	100
SHREDDED WHEAT	100g	12.3	324
(Nabisco)	each	2.5	65
SHREDDIES *(Nabisco)*	100g	10.0	375
	1oz	2.8	106
SPECIAL K *(Kelloggs)*	100g	3.9	358
	1oz	1.1	101
STARCH REDUCED	100g	15.0	345
WHEATFLAKES *(Energen)*	1oz	4.2	99
SUGAR PUFFS *(Quaker)*	100g	6.1	348
	1oz	1.7	99
SULTANA BRAN	100g	10.6	310
(Kelloggs)	1oz	3.0	88
WEETABIX	100g	12.9	380
	each (½oz)	1.8	54
WEETAFLAKES *(Weetabix)*	100g	12.9	380
	1oz	3.7	108

Food	Measure	Fibre (g)	Calories
WHOLE WHEAT FLAKES	100g	9.0	359
(Prewetts)	1oz	2.6	102
BROAD BRAN *(Allinson)*	100g	44.0	152
	1oz	12.5	43

Food	Measure	Fibre (g)	Calories
BROAD BEANS			
boiled	100g	4.2	48
	1oz	1.2	14
BROCCOLI TOPS			
raw	100g	3.6	23
	1oz	1.0	7
boiled	100g	4.1	18
	1oz	1.2	5
BRUSSELS SPROUTS			
raw	100g	4.2	26
	1oz	1.2	7
boiled	100g	2.9	18
	1oz	0.8	5
BUTTER BEANS			
raw	100g	21.6	273
	1oz	6.1	77
boiled	100g	5.1	95
	1oz	1.4	27

Food	Measure	Fibre (g)	Calories
CABBAGE			
RED, *raw*	100g	3.4	20
	1oz	1.0	6
SAVOY,			
raw	100g	3.1	26
	1oz	0.9	7
boiled	100g	2.5	9
	1oz	0.7	3
SPRING, *raw*	100g	2.2	7
	1oz	0.6	2
WHITE, *raw*	100g	2.7	22
	1oz	0.8	6
WINTER,			
raw	100g	3.4	22
	1oz	1.0	6
boiled	100g	2.8	15
	1oz	0.8	4
CAKES			
FANCY ICED	100g	2.4	407
	1oz	0.7	115

Food	Measure	Fibre (g)	Calories
FRUIT CAKE, *plain*	100g	2.8	354
	1oz	0.8	100
FRUIT CAKE, *rich*	100g	3.5	332
	1oz	1.0	94
FRUIT CAKE, *rich iced*	100g	3.4	352
	1oz	1.0	100

GINGERBREAD	100g	1.3	373
	1oz	0.4	106
JAM TARTS	100g	1.7	384
	1oz	0.5	109
MADEIRA CAKE	100g	1.4	393
	1oz	0.4	111
MINCE PIES	100g	2.9	435
	1oz	0.8	123
ROCK CAKES	100g	2.4	394
	1oz	0.7	112

Food		Measure	Fibre (g)	Calories
SCONES		100g	2.1	371
		1oz	0.6	105
SPONGE CAKE,				
	with fat	100g	1.0	464
		1oz	0.3	131
	without fat	100g	1.0	301
		1oz	0.3	85
	jam filled	100g	1.2	302
		1oz	0.4	86
CARROTS OLD,				
	raw	100g	2.9	23
		1oz	0.8	7
	boiled	100g	3.1	19
		1oz	0.9	5
YOUNG,	*boiled*	100g	3.0	20
		1oz	0.9	6
	canned	100g	3.7	19
		1oz	1.0	5
CAULIFLOWER				
raw		100g	2.1	13
		1oz	0.6	4
boiled		100g	1.8	9
		1oz	0.5	3

Food	Measure	Fibre (g)	Calories
CELERIAC			
boiled	100g	4.9	14
	1oz	1.4	4
CELERY			
raw	100g	1.8	8
	1oz	0.5	2
boiled	100g	2.2	5
	1oz	0.6	1
CHAPATIS			
made with fat	100g	3.7	336
	1oz	1.0	95
made without fat	100g	3.4	202
	1oz	1.0	57
CHERRIES			
Eating, *raw, with stones*	100g	1.5	41
	1oz	0.4	12
Cooking, *raw with stones*	100g	1.4	39
	1oz	0.4	11
stewed, with stones	100g	1.2	33
	1oz	0.3	9
Canned, *with syrup*	100g	1.0	76
	1oz	0.3	22
CHESTNUTS			
Kernels only	100g	6.8	170
	1oz	1.9	48
Weighed with shells	100g	5.7	140
	1oz	1.6	40

Food	Measure	Fibre (g)	Calories
CHICK PEAS			
raw	100g	15.0	320
	1oz	4.3	91
CHRISTMAS PUDDING	100g	2.0	304
	1oz	0.6	86
COB NUTS			
Kernels only	100g	6.1	380
	1oz	1.7	108
Weighed with shells	100g	2.2	137
	1oz	0.6	39
COCONUT			
Desiccated	100g	23.5	604
	1oz	6.7	171
Fresh	100g	13.6	351
	1oz	3.9	100
CORN FLAKES *(Kelloggs)*	100g	8.9	344
	1oz	2.5	97
CORN ON THE COB			
raw	100g	3.7	127
	1oz	1.0	36
boiled	100g	4.7	123
	1oz	1.3	35
COUNTRY STORE *(Kelloggs)*	100g	5.1	352
	1oz	1.4	100

Food	Measure	Fibre (g)	Calories
CRACKLIN' BRAN	100g	10.5	387
(Kelloggs)	1oz	3.0	110

Food	Measure	Fibre (g)	Calories
CRANBERRIES			
raw	100g	4.2	15
	1oz	1.2	4
CREAM CRACKERS	100g	3.0	440
	each	0.2	31
CRISPBREADS			
RYE, av. for most types	100g	11.7	321
	each	0.8	23
WHEAT, Starch reduced	100g	5.0	400
av. for most types	each	0.2	18
Energen			
BRANCRISP	100g	20.0	250
	each	1.3	23
Starch reduced:-			
BRAN	100g	14.0	340
	each	0.7	18
BROWNWHEAT	100g	10.0	370
	each	0.4	17

Food	Measure	Fibre (g)	Calories
CHEESE	100g	7.0	400
	each	0.3	22
RYE	100g	8.0	385
	each	0.4	18
WHEAT	100g	5.0	400
	each	0.2	18
Primula			
SUPERFINE	100g	1.4	391
	each	0.1	18
Ryvita			
ORIGINAL,	100g	11.8	315
DANISH AND SWEDISH	each	1.0	26
CRISPS	100g	11.9	533
	1 pkt (25g)	3.0	133
CUCUMBER	100g	0.4	10
	1oz	0.1	3
CURRANTS			
Dried	100g	6.5	243
	1oz	1.8	69
Black, *raw*	100g	8.7	28
	1oz	2.5	8
Red, *raw*	100g	8.2	21
	1oz	2.3	6
White, *raw*	100g	6.8	26
	1oz	1.9	7

Food	Measure	Fibre (g)	Calories
CURRANT BREAD	100g	1.7	250
	1oz	0.5	71

Food	Measure	Fibre (g)	Calories
DAMSONS			
raw	100g	3.7	34
	1oz	1.0	10
stewed	100g	3.2	29
	1oz	0.9	8
DATES			
Dried, *stoned*	100g	8.7	248
	1oz	2.5	70
Dried, *with stones*	100g	7.5	213
	1oz	2.1	60
ENDIVE	100g	2.2	11
	1oz	0.6	3
FIGS			
Fresh	100g	2.5	41
	1oz	0.7	12

Food	Measure	Fibre (g)	Calories
Dried, *raw*	100g	18.5	213
	1oz	5.2	60
stewed	100g	10.3	118
	1oz	2.9	33
FLOUR			
WHOLEMEAL 100%	100g	9.6	318
	1oz	2.7	90
BROWN 85%	100g	7.5	327
	1oz	2.1	93
WHITE 72%			
BREADMAKING	100g	3.0	337
	1oz	0.9	96
HOUSEHOLD,			
plain	100g	3.4	350
	1oz	1.0	99
self-raising	100g	3.7	339
	1oz	1.0	96

Food	Measure	Fibre (g)	Calories
Allinson			
81% FARMHOUSE			
plain	100g	8.0	351
	1oz	2.3	100
self-raising	100g	8.0	353
	1oz	2.3	100
STRONG WHITE	100g	3.0	340
	1oz	0.9	96
100% WHOLEWHEAT	100g	11.0	337
	1oz	3.1	96

Food	Measure	Fibre (g)	Calories
Prewetts			
MILLSTONE 81%			
plain	100g	8.0	340
	1oz	2.3	96
self-raising	100g	8.0	353
	1oz	2.3	100
100% WHOLEMEAL			
plain	100g	11.0	337
	1oz	3.1	96
self-raising	100g	11.0	339
	1oz	3.1	96

Food	Measure	Fibre (g)	Calories
SOYA FLOUR			
full fat	100g	11.9	447
	1oz	3.4	127
low fat	100g	14.3	352
	1oz	4.1	100
FRENCH BEANS			
boiled	100g	3.2	7
	1oz	0.9	2
FRUIT CAKE			
plain	100g	2.8	354
	1oz	0.8	100
rich	100g	3.5	332
	1oz	1.0	94
rich, iced	100g	3.4	352
	1oz	1.0	100
FRUIT SALAD			
canned	100g	1.1	95
	1oz	0.3	27
GOLDEN GRAINS	100g	5.5	376
(Prewetts)	1oz	1.6	107

Food	Measure	Fibre (g)	Calories
GOOSEBERRIES			
Green, *raw*	100g	3.2	17
	1oz	0.9	5
stewed	100g	2.7	14
	1oz	0.8	4
Ripe, *raw*	100g	3.5	37
	1oz	1.0	10
Canned, *with syrup*	100g	1.8	77
	1oz	0.5	22
GRAPES	100g	0.9	60
	1oz	0.3	17
GRAPEFRUIT			
Fresh, *whole fruit*	100g	0.3	11
	½ av. fruit (6oz)	0.5	19
flesh only	100g	0.6	22
	1oz	0.2	6
Canned, *with syrup*	100g	0.4	60
	1oz	0.1	17
GREENGAGES			
raw, weighed with stones	100g	2.5	43
	1oz	0.7	13
stewed, fruit only	100g	2.2	40
	1oz	0.6	11
stewed, weighed with stones	100g	2.1	38
	1oz	0.6	11

Food	Measure	Fibre (g)	Calories
GRAPENUTS	100g	7.0	355
(General Foods)	1oz	2.0	101
GROUNDNUTS			
Kernels only	100g	8.1	570
	1oz	2.3	162
Weighed with shells	100g	5.6	394
	1oz	1.6	112
GUAVAS			
canned, with syrup	100g	3.6	60
	1oz	1.0	17
HARICOT BEANS			
raw	100g	25.4	271
	1oz	7.2	77
boiled	100g	7.4	93
	1oz	2.1	26
HAZEL NUTS			
Kernels only	100g	6.1	380
	1oz	1.7	108
Weighed with shells	100g	2.2	137
	1oz	0.6	39
HONEY BRAN	100g	27.0	248
(Allinson)	1oz	7.6	70
HONEY MUESLI	100g	6.4	366
(Prewetts)	1oz	1.8	104

Food	Measure	Fibre (g)	Calories
HORSERADISH			
raw	100g	8.3	59
	1oz	2.4	17
sauce	100g	3.0	82
	1oz	0.9	23
JAM			
Fruit with edible seeds	100g	1.1	261
	1oz	0.3	74
Stone fruit	100g	1.0	261
	1oz	0.3	74

KIDNEY BEANS, RED			
raw	100g	25.0	272
	1oz	7.1	77
canned	100g	5.5	68
	1oz	1.6	19
LAVERBREAD	100g	3.1	52
	1oz	0.9	15

Food	Measure	Fibre (g)	Calories
LEEKS			
raw	100g	3.1	31
	1oz	0.9	9
boiled	100g	3.9	24
	1oz	1.1	7
LEMONS	100g	5.2	15
	av. fruit (4oz)	5.8	17
LENTILS			
raw	100g	11.7	304
	1oz	3.3	86
boiled	100g	3.7	99
	1oz	1.0	28
LETTUCE	100g	1.5	12
	1oz	0.4	3
LOGANBERRIES			
raw	100g	6.2	17
	1oz	1.8	5
stewed	100g	5.7	16
	1oz	1.6	5
canned	100g	3.3	101
	1oz	0.9	29
LYCHEES			
raw, flesh only	100g	0.5	64
	1oz	0.1	18
canned, with syrup	100g	0.4	68
	1oz	0.1	19

Food	Measure	Fibre (g)	Calories
MACARONI			
White, *raw*	100g	3.0	370
	1oz	0.9	105
Wholewheat, *raw*	100g	10.0	344
	1oz	2.8	97

Food	Measure	Fibre (g)	Calories
MANDARIN ORANGES			
canned, with syrup	100g	0.3	56
	1oz	0.1	16
MANGOES			
raw	100g	1.5	59
	1oz	0.4	17
canned, with syrup	100g	1.0	77
	1oz	0.3	22
MARMALADE	100g	0.7	261
	1oz	0.2	74
MARROW			
raw	100g	1.8	16
	1oz	0.5	5
boiled	100g	0.6	7
	1oz	0.2	2

Food	Measure	Fibre (g)	Calories
MARZIPAN	100g	6.4	443
	1oz	1.8	126
MATZOS	100g	3.9	384
	1oz	1.1	109
MELONS			
CANTALOUPE			
flesh only	100g	1.0	24
	1oz	0.3	7
weighed with skin	100g	0.6	15
	1oz	0.2	4
	Av. slice (8oz)	1.6	32
HONEYDEW			
flesh only	100g	0.9	21
	1oz	0.3	6
weighed with skin	100g	0.6	13
	1oz	0.2	4
	Av. slice (8oz)	1.6	32
MINCEMEAT	100g	3.3	235
	1oz	0.9	67
MINCE PIES	100g	2.9	435
	1oz	0.8	123
MUESLI	100g	7.4	368
	1oz	2.1	104
MUESLI DELUXE *(Prewetts)*	100g	7.4	390
	1oz	2.1	111

Food	Measure	Fibre (g)	Calories
MULBERRIES			
raw	100g	1.7	36
	1oz	0.5	10
MUNG BEANS			
raw	100g	22.0	231
	1oz	6.2	65
cooked, dahl	100g	6.4	106
	1oz	1.8	30
MUSHROOMS			
raw	100g	2.5	13
	1oz	0.7	4
fried	100g	4.0	210
	1oz	1.1	60
MUSTARD AND CRESS	100g	3.7	10
	1oz	1.0	3

NECTARINES	100g	2.2	46
	1oz	0.6	13
	Av. fruit (4oz)	2.4	52

Food	Measure	Fibre (g)	Calories
NUTS			
ALMONDS			
Kernels only	100g	14.3	565
	1oz	4.1	160
Weighed with shells	100g	5.3	210
	1oz	1.5	60
BARCELONA NUTS			
Kernels only	100g	10.3	639
	1oz	2.9	181
Weighed with shells	100g	6.4	396
	1oz	1.8	112
BRAZIL NUTS			
Kernels only	100g	9.0	619
	1oz	2.6	175
Weighed with shells	100g	4.1	277
	1oz	1.2	79
CHESTNUTS			
Kernels only	100g	6.8	170
	1oz	1.9	48
Weighed with shells	100g	5.7	140
	1oz	1.6	40
COB OR HAZEL NUTS			
Kernels only	100g	6.1	380
	1oz	1.7	108
Weighed with shells	100g	2.2	137
	1oz	0.6	39

Food	Measure	Fibre (g)	Calories
COCONUT			
Fresh	100g	13.6	351
	1oz	3.8	100
Desiccated	100g	23.5	604
	1oz	6.7	171
PEANUTS			
Kernels only	100g	8.1	570
	1oz	2.3	162
Weighed with shells	100g	5.6	394
	1oz	1.6	112
Roasted and salted	100g	8.1	570
	1oz	2.3	162
WALNUTS			
Kernels only	100g	5.2	525
	1oz	1.5	149
Weighed with shells	100g	3.3	336
	1oz	0.9	95

Food	Measure	Fibre (g)	Calories
OATMEAL			
raw	100g	7.0	401
	1oz	2.0	114
cooked, with water	100g	0.8	44
	1oz	0.2	12
OKRA			
raw	100g	3.2	17
	1oz	0.9	5
OLIVES, in brine			
With stones	100g	3.5	82
	1oz	1.0	23
Stoned	100g	4.4	103
	1oz	1.2	29
ONIONS			
raw	100g	1.3	23
	1oz	0.4	7
boiled	100g	1.3	13
	1oz	0.4	4
fried	100g	4.5	345
	1oz	1.3	98
Spring, *raw*	100g	3.1	35
	1oz	0.9	10
ORANGES			
Weighed with skin	100g	1.5	26
	av. fruit (5oz)	2.1	37

Food	Measure	Fibre (g)	Calories
Flesh only	100g	2.0	35
	1oz	0.5	10
PAPAYA			
Canned	100g	0.5	65
	1oz	0.1	18
PARSLEY	100g	9.1	21
	1oz	2.6	6

Food	Measure	Fibre (g)	Calories
PARSNIPS			
raw	100g	4.0	49
	1oz	1.1	14
boiled	100g	2.5	56
	1oz	0.7	16
PASSION FRUIT			
Without skin	100g	15.9	34
	1oz	4.5	10
Weighed with skin	100g	6.7	14
	1oz	1.9	4

Food	Measure	Fibre (g)	Calories
PASTA *(all shapes)*			
White, *raw*	100g	3.0	370
	1oz	0.9	105
Wholewheat, *raw*	100g	10.0	344
	1oz	2.8	97

Food	Measure	Fibre (g)	Calories
PASTRY			
Choux, *raw*	100g	0.8	214
	1oz	0.2	61
baked	100g	1.3	330
	1oz	0.4	94
Flaky, *raw*	100g	1.5	427
	1oz	0.4	121
baked	100g	2.0	565
	1oz	0.6	160
Short, *raw*	100g	2.0	455
	1oz	0.6	129
baked	100g	2.4	527
	1oz	0.7	149
PAW PAW			
Canned	100g	0.5	65
	1oz	0.1	18

Food	Measure	Fibre (g)	Calories
PEACHES			
Fresh, weighed with stone	100g	1.2	32
	1oz	0.4	9
	Av. fruit (4oz)	1.4	36
Dried, *raw*	100g	14.3	212
	1oz	4.0	60
stewed	100g	5.3	79
	1oz	1.5	22
Canned, *with syrup*	100g	1.0	87
	1oz	0.3	25
PEANUTS			
Kernels only	100g	8.1	570
	1oz	2.3	162
Weighed with shells	100g	5.6	394
	1oz	1.6	112
Roasted and salted	100g	8.1	570
	1oz	2.3	162
PEANUT BUTTER	100g	7.6	623
	1oz	2.2	177
PEARL BARLEY			
raw	100g	6.5	360
	1oz	1.8	102
boiled	100g	2.2	120
	1oz	0.6	34

Food	Measure	Fibre (g)	Calories
PEARS			
Eating	100g	1.7	29
	Av. fruit (4oz)	1.9	33
Cooking, *raw, flesh only*	100g	2.9	36
	1oz	0.8	10
stewed	100g	2.5	30
	1oz	0.7	8
Canned, *with syrup*	100g	1.7	77
	1oz	0.5	22
PEAS			
Fresh, *raw*	100g	5.2	67
	1oz	1.5	19
boiled	100g	5.2	52
	1oz	1.5	15
Frozen, *raw*	100g	7.8	53
	1oz	2.2	15
boiled	100g	12.0	41
	1oz	3.4	12
Canned, *garden*	100g	6.3	47
	1oz	1.8	13
processed	100g	7.9	80
	1oz	2.2	23
Dried, *raw*	100g	16.7	286
	1oz	4.7	81
boiled	100g	4.8	103
	1oz	1.4	29

Food	Measure	Fibre (g)	Calories
Split, dried, *raw*	100g	11.9	310
	1oz	3.4	88
boiled	100g	5.1	118
	1oz	1.4	33

PEPPERS, Green
raw	100g	0.9	15
	1oz	0.3	4
boiled	100g	0.9	14
	1oz	0.3	4

PICCALILLI
	100g	1.9	33
	1oz	0.5	9

PINEAPPLE
Fresh	100g	1.2	46
	1oz	0.3	13
Canned, *with syrup*	100g	0.9	77
	1oz	0.2	22

PLANTAINS
Green, *raw*	100g	5.8	112
	1oz	1.6	32
boiled	100g	6.4	122
	1oz	1.8	35

Food	Measure	Fibre (g)	Calories
Ripe, *fried*	100g	5.8	267
	1oz	1.6	76
PLUMS			
Dessert, *raw,*	100g	2.0	36
	1oz	0.6	10
Cooking, *raw,*	100g	2.3	23
	1oz	0.7	7
stewed,	100g	2.0	20
	1oz	0.6	6
POPCORN	100g	6.2	381
	1oz	1.8	108
PORRIDGE			
Made with water	100g	0.8	44
	1oz	0.2	12
POTATOES			
Old, *raw wt.*	100g	2.1	87
	1oz	0.6	25
baked in skin	100g	2.5	105
	1oz	0.7	30

Food	Measure	Fibre (g)	Calories
boiled	100g	1.0	80
	1oz	0.3	23
mashed	100g	0.9	119
	1oz	0.3	34
New, *boiled*	100g	2.0	76
	1oz	0.5	22
canned	100g	2.5	53
	1oz	0.7	15
Instant, *powder*	100g	16.5	318
	1oz	4.7	90
made up	100g	3.6	70
	1oz	1.0	20
Crisps	100g	11.9	533
	1 pkt (25g)	3.0	133
PRUNES			
Dried, *raw*	100g	13.4	134
	1oz	3.8	38
stewed	100g	7.4	74
	1oz	2.1	21
Canned	100g	5.1	104
	1oz	1.4	29
PUFFED WHEAT	100g	15.4	325
	1oz	4.4	92
PUMPKIN			
raw, Flesh only	100g	0.5	15
	1oz	0.1	4

Food	Measure	Fibre (g)	Calories
QUINCES			
raw, Flesh only	100g	6.4	25
	1oz	1.8	7
RADISHES	100g	1.0	15
	1oz	0.3	4
RAISINS			
Dried, stoned	100g	6.8	246
	1oz	1.9	70
RASPBERRIES			
raw	100g	7.4	25
	1oz	2.1	7
stewed	100g	7.8	26
	1oz	2.2	7
canned, with syrup	100g	5.0	87
	1oz	1.4	25
READY BREK	100g	7.6	390
	1oz	2.2	111

ood	Measure	Fibre (g)	Calories
REDCURRANTS			
raw	100g	8.2	21
	1oz	2.3	6
stewed	100g	7.0	18
	1oz	2.0	5
RED KIDNEY BEANS			
raw	100g	25.0	272
	1oz	7.1	77
canned	100g	5.5	77
	1oz	1.6	68
RHUBARB			
raw	100g	2.6	6
	1oz	0.7	2
stewed, with juice	100g	2.4	6
	1oz	0.7	2
RICE KRISPIES	100g	4.5	372
	1oz	1.3	105
RICE			
Brown, *raw*	100g	5.0	340
	1oz	1.4	96
White, *raw*	100g	2.4	361
	1oz	0.6	102
boiled	100g	0.8	123
	1oz	0.2	35
Uncle Ben's Easy Cook Rice	100g	0.3	357
	1oz	0.1	101

Food	Measure	Fibre (g)	Calories
RUNNER BEANS			
raw	100g	2.9	26
	1oz	0.8	7
boiled	100g	3.4	19
	1oz	1.0	5
RYVITA			
Original, Danish,	100g	11.8	315
Swedish types	per slice	1.0	26

Food	Measure	Fibre (g)	Calories
SEAKALE, stems			
boiled	100g	1.2	8
	1oz	0.3	2.3
SHREDDED WHEAT	100g	12.3	324
	each	2.5	65
SHREDDIES	100g	10.0	375
	1oz	2.8	106
SODA BREAD	100g	2.3	264
	1oz	0.7	75
SOYA FLOUR			
Full fat	100g	11.9	447
	1oz	3.4	127

ood	Measure	Fibre (g)	Calories
Low fat	100g	14.3	352
	1oz	4.1	100
PAGHETTI			
White, *raw*	100g	3.0	370
	1oz	0.9	105
Wholewheat, *raw*	100g	10.0	344
	1oz	2.8	97
PECIAL K *(Kelloggs)*	100g	3.9	358
	1oz	1.1	101
PINACH			
boiled	100g	6.3	30
	1oz	1.8	9
canned	100g	5.0	20
	1oz	1.4	6
PLIT PEAS, *dried*			
raw	100g	11.9	310
	1oz	3.4	88
boiled	100g	5.1	118
	1oz	1.4	33
PRING GREENS			
boiled	100g	3.8	10
	1oz	1.1	3
PRING ONIONS			
raw	100g	3.1	35
	1oz	0.9	10

Food	Measure	Fibre (g)	Calorie
SPROUTS			
raw	100g	4.2	26
	1oz	1.2	7
boiled	100g	2.9	18
	1oz	0.8	5
STRAWBERRIES			
Fresh	100g	2.2	26
	1oz	0.6	7
canned, with syrup	100g	1.0	81
	1oz	0.3	23
SUGAR PUFFS _(Quaker)_	100g	6.1	348
	1oz	1.7	99
SULTANAS	100g	7.0	250
	1oz	2.0	71
SULTANA BRAN	100g	10.6	310
(Kelloggs)	1oz	3.0	88
SWEDES			
raw	100g	2.7	21
	1oz	0.8	6
boiled	100g	2.8	18
	1oz	0.8	5
SWEETCORN			
On the cob, _raw_	100g	3.7	127
	1oz	1.0	36

ood	Measure	Fibre (g)	Calories
boiled	100g	4.7	123
	1oz	1.3	35
Kernels, *canned*	100g	5.7	76
	1oz	1.6	22

WEET POTATOES

raw	100g	2.5	91
	1oz	0.7	26
boiled	100g	2.3	85
	1oz	0.7	24

ANGERINES

Flesh only	100g	1.9	34
	1oz	0.5	10
Whole fruit	100g	1.3	23
	Av. fruit (3oz)	1.1	20

OMATOES

Fresh, *raw*	100g	1.5	14
	1oz	0.4	4
fried	100g	3.0	69
	1oz	0.8	20
Canned, *strained*	100g	0.9	12
	1oz	0.3	3

Food	Measure	Fibre (g)	Calorie
TURNIPS			
raw	100g	2.8	20
	1oz	0.8	6
boiled	100g	2.2	14
	1oz	0.6	4
TURNIP TOPS			
boiled	100g	3.9	11
	1oz	1.1	3

Food	Measure	Fibre (g)	Calorie
WALNUTS			
Kernels only	100g	5.2	525
	1oz	1.5	149
Weighed with shells	100g	3.3	336
	1oz	0.9	95
WATERCRESS			
raw	100g	3.3	14
	1oz	0.9	4
WEETABIX	100g	12.9	380
	1oz	3.7	107
	each	1.8	54